TOM BRADY

SUPERSTAR QUARTERBACK

BIG BUDDY

NFL SUPERSTARS

Big Buddy Books
An Imprint of Abdo Publishing
abdobooks.com

DENNIS ST. SAUVER

abdobooks.com

Published by Abdo Publishing, a division of ABDO, PO Box 398166, Minneapolis, Minnesota 55439. Copyright © 2020 by Abdo Consulting Group, Inc. International copyrights reserved in all countries. No part of this book may be reproduced in any form without written permission from the publisher. Big Buddy Books™ is a trademark and logo of Abdo Publishing.

Printed in the United States of America, North Mankato, Minnesota.
052019
092019

THIS BOOK CONTAINS RECYCLED MATERIALS

Cover Photo: efks/Getty Images; Maddie Meyer/Getty Images.
Interior Photos: Carlos Osorio/AP Images (p. 13); David Joles/Minneapolis Star Tribune/ZUMA Wire/ Alamy Stock Photo (p. 9); Doug Pensinger/Getty Images (p. 19); Ezra Shaw/Getty Images (p. 15); Handout/Getty Images (p. 25); Jamie Squire/Getty Images (p. 27); Jim Rogash/Getty Images (p. 17); Maddie Meyer/Getty Images (p. 5); Mike Ehrmann/Getty Images (p. 29); Scott Boehm/AP Images (p. 11); Stephen Dunn/Getty Images (p. 23); Tom Pennington/Getty Images (p. 21).

Coordinating Series Editor: Elizabeth Andrews
Graphic Design: Jenny Christensen, Cody Laberda

Library of Congress Control Number: 2018967161

Publisher's Cataloging-in-Publication Data

Names: St. Sauver, Dennis, author.
Title: Tom Brady: superstar quarterback / by Dennis St. Sauver
Other title: superstar quarterback
Description: Minneapolis, Minnesota : Abdo Publishing, 2020 | Series: NFL superstars | Includes online resources and index.
Identifiers: ISBN 9781532119781 (lib. bdg.) | ISBN 9781532174544 (ebook)
Subjects: LCSH: Brady, Tom, 1977---Juvenile literature. | Football players--United States--Biography--Juvenile literature. | Quarterbacks (Football)--United States-- Biography--Juvenile literature. | New England Patriots (Football team)--Juvenile literature.
Classification: DDC 796.3326409 [B]--dc23

8/19

CONTENTS

★ ★ ★ ★ ★ ★

SUPERSTAR QUARTERBACK

Tom Brady is a star quarterback in the National Football League (NFL). He plays for the New England Patriots in Massachusetts. Tom has won six Super Bowl **Championships**. Many think he is the best quarterback in football history.

DID YOU KNOW?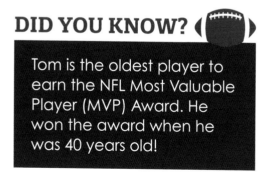

Tom is the oldest player to earn the NFL Most Valuable Player (MVP) Award. He won the award when he was 40 years old!

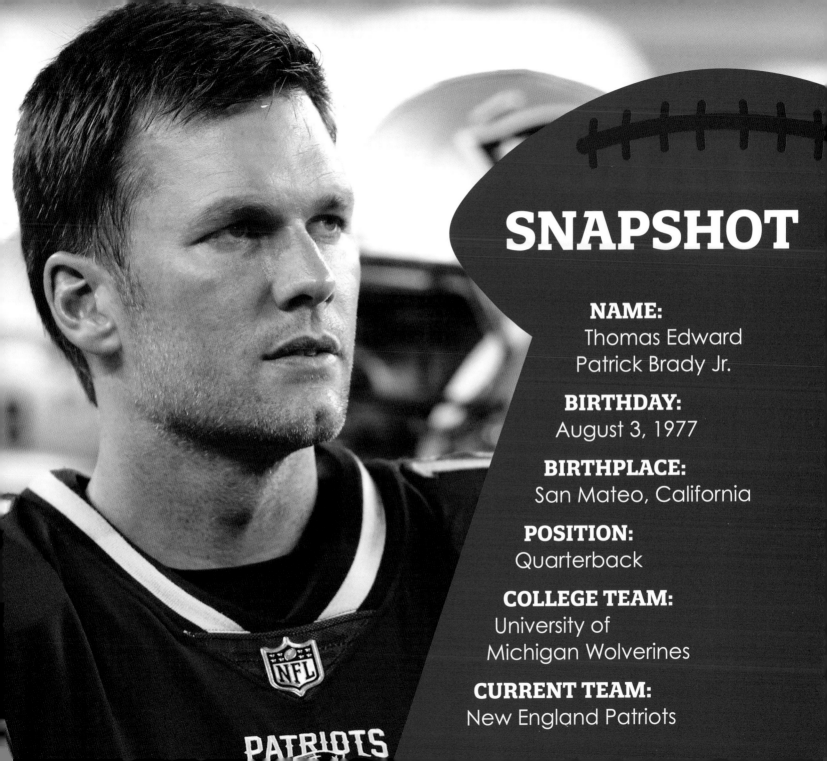

SNAPSHOT

NAME:
Thomas Edward
Patrick Brady Jr.

BIRTHDAY:
August 3, 1977

BIRTHPLACE:
San Mateo, California

POSITION:
Quarterback

COLLEGE TEAM:
University of
Michigan Wolverines

CURRENT TEAM:
New England Patriots

EARLY YEARS

Tom is the youngest child of Thomas and Galynn Brady. He has three sisters named Nancy, Julie, and Maureen.

Growing up, Tom enjoyed baseball and football. He was also a fan of the Los Angeles Lakers and Boston Celtics basketball teams.

In elementary school, Tom played football at recess. He was often the quarterback.

Where was Tom Brady born?

CANADA

UNITED STATES OF AMERICA

MEXICO

Oregon

Nevada

San Mateo

California

Arizona

Pacific Ocean

MEXICO

N
W E
S

STARTING OUT

★

In high school, Tom played baseball and football. He was the quarterback for his football team during his junior and senior years.

At practice, he worked on his speed to become a better player. Tom's coaches were proud of how hard he worked to improve his skills.

Growing up, Tom and his sisters played basketball and football together on Sunday afternoons.

Tom was also an excellent baseball player. A **professional** baseball team called the Montreal Expos **drafted** him in 1995. He had to decide between playing football or baseball.

Tom's football hero was Joe Montana, a star quarterback for the San Francisco 49ers. Tom wanted to be a quarterback like Joe. So he decided to attend college on a football **scholarship**. He picked the University of Michigan and soon became a star.

DID YOU KNOW?

Tom went to the same high school as professional baseball player Barry Bonds.

In college, Tom played as number 10 for the University of Michigan. He plays as number 12 for the Patriots.

BIG DREAMS

Tom did not get to play much until his third year of college. That season, Tom **passed** for 2,427 yards (2,219 m). That is great for a quarterback. His team shared the 1998 Big Ten Football **Championship title** with Ohio State and Wisconsin.

Tom studied hard in college and got very good grades. He also worked a construction job and at a golf course.

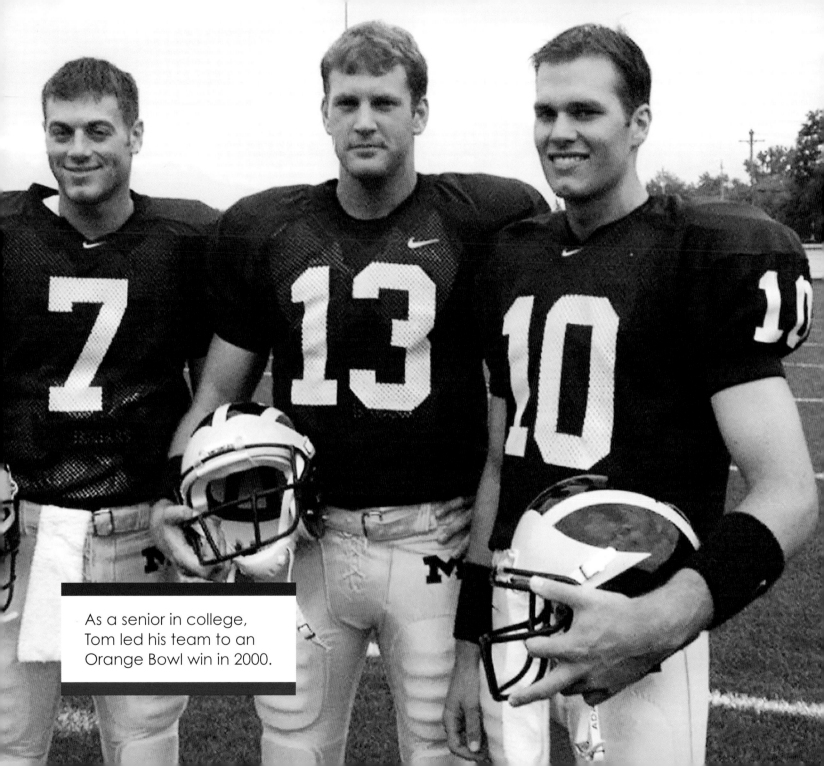

As a senior in college, Tom led his team to an Orange Bowl win in 2000.

GOING PRO

The New England Patriots **drafted** Tom in 2000. He was not picked until the sixth round, which is very low. Tom surprised everyone by becoming one of the best quarterbacks of all time!

In Tom's second year, he led his team to 11 wins and a Super Bowl victory. Two years later, he helped the Patriots to another Super Bowl win.

Tom has a few different nicknames. Some people call him Terrific Tom, Touchdown Tom, or The Pharaoh (fehr-oh).

Before Tom joined the Patriots, the team was not very strong on the field. It was near the bottom of its **division** from 1998 to 2000. The Patriots won 22 games, but lost 26 during those three seasons.

Once Coach Bill Belichick made Tom the starter in 2001, things changed. The team began winning every year. Since then, the Patriots team has won its division 16 out of 18 seasons.

Tom has played for the New England Patriots his entire professional career.

A RISING STAR

The Patriots team is one of the best in the league. And Tom is one of the reasons. His hard work and positive **attitude** help him become a better player each year.

Tom is very smart and spends time studying football. He then makes changes to improve his game.

In 2007, the Patriots did not lose a single regular-season game. Sadly, the New York Giants beat the Patriots in the Super Bowl.

Tom was **injured** in 2008 and missed the entire year. Some thought his **career** was over, but he proved all of them wrong. When he came back, he went on to win three more Super Bowls!

Tom has won more regular-season and **playoff** games than any other quarterback in NFL history. And he has been in more playoff games than any player at any position. Tom has **passed** for more than 70,000 yards (64,008 m) in his career!

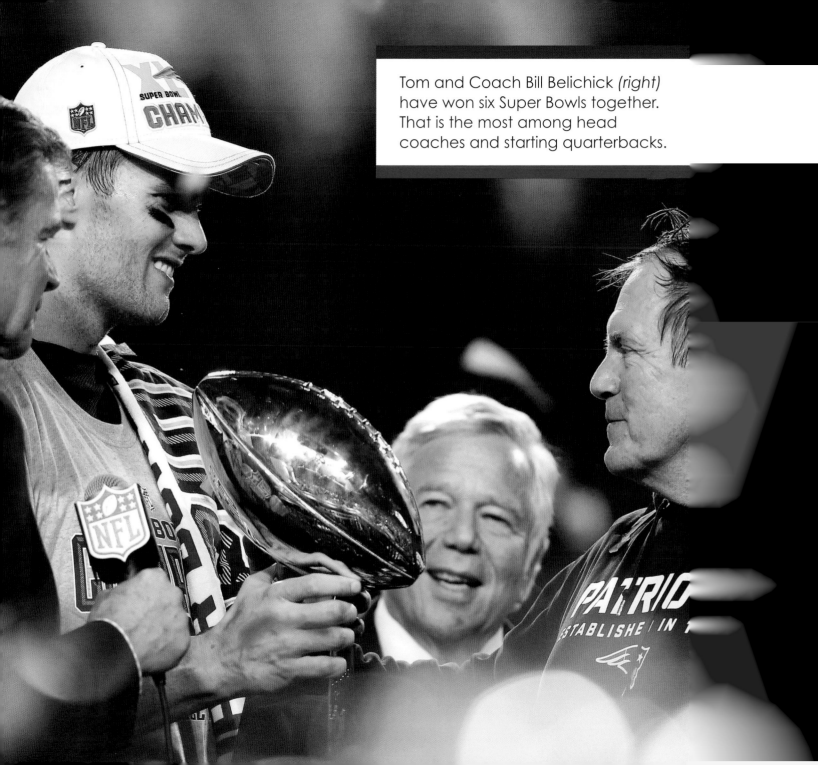

Tom and Coach Bill Belichick (right) have won six Super Bowls together. That is the most among head coaches and starting quarterbacks.

OFF THE FIELD

Tom is married to Gisele Bündchen, a supermodel from Brazil. They have two children together, Benjamin and Vivian. Tom also has an older son named John. Tom and his family live in Massachusetts and love spending time together.

DID YOU KNOW?

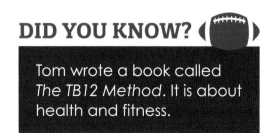

Tom wrote a book called *The TB12 Method*. It is about health and fitness.

In their free time, Tom and Gisele are very interested in staying fit and healthy. Tom enjoys playing golf and has even tried surfing.

GIVING BACK

While Tom is a great football player, he is also a very caring person. He plays a big part in the Best Buddies International **organization**. This group **supports** people with special needs.

Tom works with many other groups too. Some include the Boys and Girls Clubs of America and KaBOOM! He and Gisele have been very **generous** in giving back to the community.

In 2015, Tom gave $50,000 to the Jimmy Fund. This organization supports cancer care and research.

AWARDS

Tom is a six-time Super Bowl **champion**, all with the New England Patriots. The Patriots took second place three other times during Tom's **career**. He was the starting quarterback in each of those games.

Tom has earned four Super Bowl **MVP** awards, and three regular-season MVP awards. And he has been named to the **Pro Bowl** 14 times!

In his 18 years as a starting quarterback, Tom has never had a losing season.

BUZZ

In August 2018, Tom signed a contract that will pay him a lot of money to continue playing in the NFL. He wants to play for a few more seasons. Fans hope he will stay in the NFL and continue to help the Patriots win!